CHEEKY JURGEN'S
Book of Cheeky Sayings

WINK

THE STORY OF THE ACCIDENTAL BIRTH AND CREATION OF CHEEKY JURGEN

A fully interactive book experience from the social media sensation @cheekyjurgen

Mereo Books

2nd Floor, 6-8 Dyer Street, Cirencester, Gloucestershire, GL7 2PF
An imprint of Memoirs Books. www.mereobooks.com
and www.memoirsbooks.co.uk

Cheeky Jurgen's Book of Cheeky Sayings
ISBN: 978-1-86151-644-2

First published in Great Britain in 2021
by Mereo Books, an imprint of Memoirs Books.
Copyright ©2021

All cartoons produced by Josh Knowles

The address for Memoirs Books can be
found at www.mereobooks.com

Mereo Books Ltd. Reg. No. 12157152

Typeset in Aktiv Grotesk
by Wiltshire Associates.
Printed and bound in Great Britain

QR Codes

This book is much more than printed words on paper – just scan each QR code as you come to it with your tablet, Android or iPhone and you will be taken straight to a video or sound clip. In case your tablet or phone doesn't have a QR code scan app enabled it can be downloaded free from Google Play.

Foreword

So this is for Jurgen Klopp's autobiography ja? But there again, don't ask me - what do I know. Cheeky Jurgen had me but no one really noticed did they?!

What started as a cheeky selfie to tease a mate who is a Liverpool fan suddenly became a global talking point where I was the one on the receiving end of being teased. I laughed about it then and still do now.

After 20 years of broadcasting from war zones to world cups one of the things I'm asked about is....did you know it was Cheeky Jurgen?

Well I do now. At the time 'Jurgen' was being stopped for selfies near the VIP entrance at Wembley as England were about to take on Germany in the quarter-finals of the Euros. I don't normally ask for selfies but I was excited about the match, 'Jurgen' was standing right there happily posing with other fans, he seemed approachable, so why not.

Talking about it on the telly the next day was perhaps not the best idea but great for 'Cheeky Jurgen'. His popularity escalated from posts on social media to mainstream media and not just in the UK but even around the world it seemed everyone loved a story about an experienced TV Correspondent being fooled by a Jurgen look-a-like. I read the articles and had a good laugh about it myself, friends were calling up crying with laughter and finally they'd admit but 'yeah he does look like him'.

He's got the teeth, the hair and the accent and if asked he could probably pick a decent football team too. Fair play Ray.

Enjoy the book but it's the last time I ask any managers for a selfie Ja.

JONATHAN SWAIN - SENIOR NEWS CORRESPONDENT
GOOD MORNING BRITAIN
ITV BREAKFAST TELEVISION

TWITTER: @SWAINITV
EMAIL: jonathan.swain@itv.com
WEB: https://www.itv.com/goodmorningbritain/jonathan-swain

Introduction

This is the amazing story of how my five-year-old granddaughter, Annabella, changed my life and those of many people around me by making a comment when she happened to see the great Jurgen Klopp on TV during a football match. She asked: "Pappi, Pappi" (Grandad), "why are you always on the TV?"

Her confused look brought a smile to my face, and instantly I understood what this meant. At that moment, the idea of Cheeky Jurgen was born.

Little did Annabella realise that after giving life to the idea of Cheeky Jurgen, she would herself be on Breakfast TV the following year helping a film crew at Cheeky Jurgen's country house at 5 am! All will be revealed later.

KICK OFF AT ANFIELD

Let The Beautiful Game Begin!

Jurgen is a-coming, meine Schmusebears*, ja!

*This means (more or less) 'my lovely cuddly bears'

Hear Cheeky Jurgen's dulcet tones and amazing German accent on the homepage of his website.

The genesis of Cheeky Jurgen: How to create a
Kloppelganger

First things first: we need the BIG TEETH. Without the teeth, there is no Jurgen.

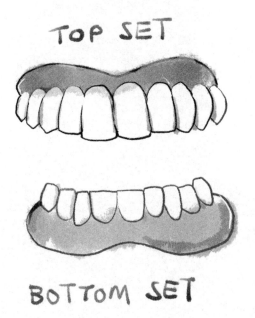

TOP SET

BOTTOM SET

A chance meeting at a favourite local pub (the Crown in Bloomsbury, London) with a total stranger who overheard us talking about the Jurgen project led us to Fangs FX theatrical and film dental veneer specialists in Amersham. Now we were in business!

But then… Covid struck.
No pubs – no 'time Jurgen please'.
No fans to adore me.
No football.
Nothing to live for!
The end of life as we knew it!!!

(And definitely no shops open to complete Jurgen's extensive wardrobe)

But there is always a way to spend cheeky money...

ONLINE!

We ordered puffer jackets, shirts, socks, caps, trainers and typical (but lovely) Scouser trackie bottoms...

We got hold of Jurgen's exact glasses (from Oakley) and some dazzling blue contact lenses.

We were now ready to rock n' roll.

But suddenly we were in the middle of a bloody
LOCKDOWN!

LESSONS FROM LOCKDOWN
Gegenpressing!

Cheeky Jurgen says: Scheisse! With zese stupid Covid rules, It's bloody difficult to do ze gegenpressing, also known as heavy metal football, ja?

What is *Gegenpressing*? It is Jurgen Klopp's ideology of football. Gegenpressing ('pressing against') means to press the opposition straight after losing possession, i.e. to press as an organized unit the moment you transition to defence.

'Heavy metal football' is a term coined by Jurgen Klopp, and it describes a type of play characterised by high pressing, quick passing and a very hard work rate. It is an in-your-face type of football – fast, aggressive, passionate and exciting. But you still use boots - you never throw guitars or drums around. At least, in most countries.

Cheeky Jurgen says:

"

Zen after ze footie, what is going to happen with my boys in zat big, big bath? Why do zay love to spend so much time in ze bath together?

"

As Vanity Von Glow says, rub a dub dub, eleven men in a tub...

Watch the full interview here

In the depths of Covid lockdown, Cheeky Jurgen was so, so sad. He had nothing to do but watch his lovely red Liverpool paint dry, stir his coffee clockwise instead of anticlockwise and work the indicators on his beloved Rover P5B.

Strange but true.
You can watch all of zese videos here.

Then at last there came a light at the end
of the Covid tunnel.

For the last match of the season, fans
were finally allowed back into Anfield.

After a strong start to the season but a mixed run
of form, Liverpool - the defending Premier League
Champions – needed a win to qualify for the top
four and the Champions League.

Step up: The Eagles – Crystal Palace
– and of course, Cheeky Jurgen...

Before the match Cheeky Jurgen was out and about meeting all the fans and causing crazy confusion. They really thought Cheeky Jurgen was Jurgen Klopp. They were chanting along with him in the Anfield Road and even doing the famous fist pump together.

Suddenly a guy called Neil from DTBTV (Doubt To Believers TV) shoved a red flare into Cheeky Jurgen's hand and the moment went viral. Millions of views within hours all over the world...

'A flare to hold in the Anfield Road, big and red, and very very bold.'

Zo back to ze final match: Liverpool v Palace!

Cheeky Jurgen says:

"

Ze Eagles are coming here, meine Schmusebears, und I promise you ve vill clip zere wings und zay vill play like bloody turkeys, ja?

"

(And they did – 2-0 to the Reds.)

Zo after the match a party was had by all at the Sandon Hotel. And boy was it a party. A bit of a train crash celebration actually, but hey, a result is a result.

Cheeky Jurgen is feeling a little tipsy
at ze moment!

"

Zo I am gunna ask ze question: Meine Schmusebears, have you ever been Kloppelganged? (It doesn't hurt, does it?) If zo, when, where, and how?"

"

(Now, now boys und girls please
keep ze answers clean)!

Write it here to keep it private or tweet
us to make it public!

#cheekyjurgen

Cheeky Jurgen says:

"

Und zo, now Liverpool are back in ze Champions' League, I have eine little joke for you before we even tackle ze very special subject of Mourinho….

"

Why do pigeons fly upside down
over Old Trafford?

Because it is not worth crapping on!

And now to the Special One!

In fact, considering that the Special One has managed zo many different clubs in such a short space of time, Cheeky Jurgen is considering nominating him for a leading Environmental Award because he has been recycled zo many bloody times. (Apparently this will leave a lower carbon footprint, and help in the fight against global warming).

Cheeky Jurgen says:

"

You know what? Although ze Special One is not zo special anymore, I do take him out for ze dinner from time to time at my favourite German restaurant. And I tell you, when we dine together, I always like to order him a big plate of SCHADENFREUDE (that means taking pleasure in someone else's pain).

"

SCHADENFREUDE: a dish best served kalt (cold). What do you think a plate of it really looks like?

DRAW IT HERE

Und by ze way, vair iss his old club? Tottten-ham? Is zat even in London? I'm not zo sure you know. Anyway, I zink it's not a very big club, ja? Sometimes he even cries like a baby! But zen I send him ze Kleenex for a gute Christmas.

Ok, zo before ve start talking about my favourite Liverpool players, there is a little secret I have to let you in on…

I have a **BIG SCHLOSS!**

Yes, Cheeky Jurgen has a

VERY BIG SCHLOSS.

Turn the page to find out more…

Und – by ze vay – my Schloss or holiday chalet **(I don't know what you were thinking)** is in the French Alps. Briançon – 300 days of sun a year and one of the most beautiful places in the world. (Mein Schloss could be your gain).

You can check it out here:

Q: **They always say that the French are zo lazy. Zo why is it that they like to eat the snails zo much?**

A: **Because it's the only bloody thing they can catch ja!**

UND ZO, NOW TO ZE PLAYERS…

Zo, Flamingo/Firminio. After seeing your lovely new teeth, my dear Roberto, I was zo, zo jealous, zo I sank you zo zwo much for the idea to get my teeth done as well! Now with both of our teeth like zis, in ze dark, We'll Never Walk Alone.

And now we need to talk about the big, famous M. Zo a BIG thank you to the Egyptian people for Mo Farah.

Ze Eqyptian King;
Ze Football Pharaoh;

Of course – Mohammed Salah from the beautiful village of Nagrig.

Both are amazing athletes –
I sink I shcrewed it up, ja?

As seen on Egyptian TV Ontime Sports

THE EGYPTIAN KING

Point of order for the record:

Cheeky Jurgen would like to thank the management and directors of Chelsea FC zo much for keeping the Big M in such a key position whilst (playing?) for them.

And now moving on to a medical journal for Jurgen!

We know the hair implants have been done, the teeth have had veneers and now the rumours have been confirmed that he has had eye surgery but what is next?

What else should Jurgen get done?

(Keep it clean now, boys and girls – remember I already have a big schloss!)

Send your answers to: #cheekyjurgen

Zo Cheeky Jurgen hits the road
and meets zo many lovely
interesting schmuse-bears and even
ein schmuse-dog.

Jurgen meets his SCHMUSE–DOG!

And zo now Cheeky Jurgen meets the Jurgen cardboard cut-out in the Anfield Road.

Cheeky Jurgen wants to know, zo who do you sink is ze prettiest and ze Jurgenest?

I am sinking of how to negotiate ze use of this image, because now according to many experts (and even TV presenters, ha ha), I am looking more like Jurgen zan bloody Jurgen!

Jurgen meets Richard ('the Hamster')
Hammond from Top Gear and the
Grand Tour at the London Classic Car
Show 2021.

You know, he's not zat small, it's just zat
I'm REALLY, REALLY TALL.

Also at ze Classic Car Show – Cheeky Jurgen met ze great motorsport presenter Tiff Needell. He had a tough tit for tat tiff with Tiff in Tiff's tent. After a great interview covering many topics, Tiff was needled. Ze conversation turned ominously to the subject of football. Tiff was adamant that he needed his Southampton players back… and blows were almost exchanged.

Still at the London Classic Car Show,
Cheeky Jurgen was in his BIG BLACK
DODGE CHARGER – The Beefy American
Meat Car!

Cheeky Jurgen says: !

"

**Und I tell you this proves the point
that size really does matter, meine
Schmuse-bears!**

"

Q: Cheeky Jurgen and the guys at the Afro Classic Register want to know why the Japanese don't make popular classic cars.

A:

1) Because Japanese cars are reliable.
2) Because they don't leak.
3) Because they don't rust.
4) Because they never break down.
5) Because they don't constantly need repairing.

Cheeky Jurgen says:

"

Zis is a really gut excuse for escaping ze missus (or ze mister, it depends)... because you can be under ze bonnet for countless hours at times of your choice with no explanations

"

But let me tell you another little secret, ja? Cheeky Jurgen has a collection of beautiful, old Britisch classic cars. Zo if you wanna have some fun driving see the link below:

Again a big sank you to all ze guys at ze Afro Classics Register. (The Jerk Chicken was amazing).

Ok Cheeky Jurgen (or the fans' nickname for him, The Kloppelganger) pays a visit to Anfield and The Kop. Und one of the things I noticed first vos zat ze grass is as schmoooth as a baby's bottom!

Before Cheeky Jurgen sits in Jurgen's hot seat for the very first time he makes sure his hands are clean and sanitised, just like ze doctor ordered, ja?

Und ja, zese hands are really, really clean because we don't want to break any of those rules, meine Schmuse-bears!

Mein Gott, look at ze size of Cheeky Jurgen's big, big trophies!

What a pair of beauties, ja? Und as I said before, size really does matter. Ze Crown Jewels, as I sink zey say in English!

Cheeky Jurgen says:

"

To all ze Liverpool boys und girls out zere, let's work togezzer to bring zese beautiful big cups back to Anfield where zey belong.

"

Outside Anfield, after the inspection of that oh zo beautiful and wonderful stadium, Cheeky Jurgen was suddenly accosted by a TOFFEE.

Cheeky Jurgen says:

"

Zose bloody toffees get everywhere, zey schtick in your teeth and make zem fall out! Does anyone know what zay are bloody good for? (But sanks anyway to him for having such a good laugh togezzer and being a bloody gut schport).

"

You know what? Zey say zat ze Germans don't have a sense of humour (and I think they might be right there) but Cheeky Jurgen definitely does, ja?

Turn the pages for some of Cheeky Jurgen's Favourite Funnies reflecting on the bitter but respected rivalry between the two most successful teams ever in English football history and far, far beyond...

CHEEKY JURGEN'S
FAVOURITE FUNNIES

I left two MUFC tickets in my E-type yesterday. Someone smashed the window and left two more.

MUFC have set up a call centre for fans who are troubled by their current form. The number is 0800 10 10 10. To make that easy to remember, it's '0800 won nothing won nothing won nothing'

Q: **What have MUFC and a three-pin plug got in common?**

A: **They are both bugger all use in Europe.**

There is a new drinking game in town that you can play, you can only take a shot when Man United do. It's called Dry January.

Q: What has Old Trafford on a Saturday afternoon at 4.45pm got in common with Wormwood Scrubs Prison?

A: They are both full of cockneys trying to get out.

A little girl was making a Christmas wish with Santa.

She said "I would like a unicorn for Christmas". Santa replies, "but unicorns are just imaginary – make another wish". She says ok, I would like Manchester United to win the league."

Santa replied, "what colour unicorn would you like?"

Q: **What do you get when you offer a Man United fan a penny for their thoughts?**

A: **Change.**

Q: **What do MUFC fans use as birth control?**

A: **Their personalities.**

AND NOW A FEW REALLY CHEEKY ONES FROM CHEEKY JURGEN'S PRIVATE COLLECTION:

Q: **You are trapped in a room with a tiger, a rattlesnake and a Man United fan and you have a gun loaded with only two bullets – what should you do?**

A: **Shoot the Man United fan twice.**

Q: **What is the difference between a Man United fan and a vibrator?**

A: **A Man United fan is a real dick.**

Q: **Did you hear that the Post Office just recalled their latest stamps?**

A: **They had pictures of Man United players on them, and people couldn't figure out which side to spit on.**

Und now to ze second half… and hopefully ve don't have to play ze extra bloody time!

How Cheeky Jurgen fooled the world...

Zo Cheeky Jurgen went to Wembley and fooled ze world's press: German, British, Israeli and Arab TV, radio and social media. Already on the Unterground to see England vs Germany, he was causing a big, big schtirrr.......

Und zo we leave ze Unterground and walk to ze stadium und on Wembley Way, guess who comes up to me wiz an English accent with his big film crew for a quick cheeky interview? It was… It was…
To be honest I have no bloody idea who he vas.
Can you guess why?
We had COVID remember! Zo he was wearing a MASK!

We finished the interview and he says **'Goodbye Jurgen'**. 'Goodbye mysterious mask-wearing interviewer,' I say.

Who ze bloody hell vas zat?

Outside the stadium, the lovely crazy English fans are chanting JURGEN! JURGEN! JURGEN! Then this butch, strong man puts his head between my legs.

O mein Gott, I zink I am being gegenpressed for ze first time in my life!

Cheeky Jurgen wants to know: To all ze boys und girls out zere und meine Schmuse-bears all over the world, have you ever been gegenpressed in your life?

If zo, where?
When?
How?
Tell Cheeky! #cheekyjurgen

Boys and girls, please keep ze answers clean, but if you can't, make zem really, really DIRTY!

SWINK

AND THEN...

This big, butch, strong fan stands up and Jurgen is on his shoulders, suddenly above all the crowd. Everyone goes really crazy, a beer can is thrust into his hands and the rest, as they say, is history. The video goes viral and within two hours it is all over ze world with 3.5 million views, even getting as far as SPORTbible in Australia. Can you believe zat?!

Zo zen ze media floodgates really opened. Good Morning Britain and BBC Radio Five Live both wanted me to do an interview about ze successful blag I had unwittingly played on Jonathan Swain.

Cheeky Jurgen says:

"

I zink as you say in English, ze poor guy had ze egg on face ja?

"

Zo really, from ze bottom of my cheeky cheeky heart I sank Mr Swain zo, zo much for making zis blunder (which was understandable as I am ze best Jurgen Klopp lookalike in ze whole world). Now everysing turned mental, turbo, crazy busy. Cheeky Jurgen was launched onto the world's stage.

The more memorable highlights from my 15 minutes of fame include appearing on BBC Radio Five with Nicky Campbell asking some very, very Cheeky questions. Then there was a fantastic long discussion about Cheeky Jurgen on the Frank Skinner breakfast show on Absolute Radio questioning whether the whole thing was a set up or not. Zo zo funny!

And finally I think the best of them all was The Last Leg on Channel 4. OMG that was such fun. Genuinely good banter.

Cheeky Jurgen wants to know:

Why did zay suddenly srow me off ze stage when zay realised I was ze real Cheeky Jurgen? Why? Why? Why? I need a job, I need ze money!

SEE POLL BELOW!

There is still time to take part in their poll:

If Cheeky Jurgen was a euphemism, what would it be a euphemism for?

Let Cheeky know at #cheekyjurgen

Which leads us to ze schticky subject of ze English press! Ze interviews were such great fun, but after a while it was clear zat ze press likes just a little bit, meine Schmuse-bears, to exaggerate. I have told zem a million times to stop exaggerating! Zay also sometimes get zere facts wrong. Zis is not like ze German press, which is always zo korrekt! Zo, ze first day's coverage in ze press went sumsing like zis:

9 am:
Successful businessman, 6'4"

12 noon:
Successful and very rich business man, 5'11"

3 pm:
Eccentric millionaire, 5'6"

6 pm:
Multi Millionaire Tycoon, 5'1"

9 pm:
Multi billionaire champagne swilling plutocratic oligarch. officially now a midget

Zo ze big lesson in life is:
For God's sake don't rely on the
press for the truth and definitely

NO BLOODY
PAPARAZZI!

CHEEKY JURGEN
MAYBE

JURGEN KLOPP
MAYBE

OK! Zo to all my Liverpool boys und girls and all my schmuse-bears all around ze world we must tackle a very schticky subject:

ZE BLOODY VAR

You must never mention ze VAR!

But what is zis VAR, I hear you ask?

Very Annoying Referee?
Very Argumentative Results?
Vicious Automated Robot?

What do you think V.A.R. stands for? Tell us at #cheekyjurgen (Any answers must pass FIFA's PC Police but please, no filth… ok maybe just a little bit)

Cheeky Jurgen's Top Three Euro Moments

Undoubtedly the result that brought the biggest schmile to meine face was schtuffing ze German schnitzels 2-0. This was ze wurst result for them in many years. Das is sehr gut, ja!

Everyone was wondering why is Jurgen, a proud and noble German, supporting ze English? But I zink we all know ze real answer to zat, don't we meine schmuse-bears!

Und now zings were getting really exciting. A semi-final place with ze Danish. Ze Danish, we all love ze Danish – zey are such cool and happy people, but you know, secretly I call zem ze bacons, ze bacons, ze bloody Danish bacons. And you know what we do with ze bacons?

We fry zem and have zem for breakfast. And we certainly did

SCHNURF

SCHNIFFEL

Und zo to ze big, big one, ja? England's first football final for fünf und fünfzig Jahren! Zat's 55 years. And as Cheeky Jurgen said – bring on ze Italians. I must admit I sought wiz ze heat and ze pressure from ze English zay will melt just like ze mozzarella on one of zeir pizzas.

For most of ze game I was right. I really sought we played ze better fussball, but at ze end of ze day Mancini was ein better tactician.

Ze prime example of zis was ze PENALTIES. What ze f… could possibly go wrong wiz eine Britische team kicking ze penalties, I hear you ask? Surely zey could not miss?

Zis is one page where Cheeky Jurgen is going to show his SERIOUS SIDE. Und zis is his question:

Wiz some of ze best players in the world available, why did zey choose a 19-year-old *Junge* who came on as a substitute and had never taken a professional penalty in his life? To put ze weight of expectation of the whole nation on his young shoulders to me seems inexplicable – **although he did have the balls to step up to the challenge.**

I am zo, zo sorry, you sought I said It was coming home zis time. But I sink you misunderstood. Wiz my bad English accent, I cannot pronounce ze R ze way you Britisch do.

I meant "It's coming, ROME!"

Cheeky Jurgen says:

"

But ze English team did us proud in getting zo far – let's not forget zat.

(Please don't forget we stuffed ze Schnitzels and in anyone's books zat's a result to be proud of!) England played zo well and next time, for sure, we will go all ze way.

"

Now for ze zukunft – sorry zat's 'future' in English, but it's a nice word, ja? I sink I will use it again. But you must be careful never to address a person wiz it ('Hey, ZUKUNFT!') or you might wake up to find yourself in, how you say, ein intensive care unit.

For *ze zukunft*, Cheeky Jurgen's TOP TIPS for all ze England penalty takers. Listen to me, zis is extremely important. I will say it only twice.

To score a goal, zere are SREE sings you really must get right:

Look at ze page opposite find out…

1) Place ze Ball (ze Geman word for ball) between you and ze Netz (ze German word for net).

2) Schwing ze leg (it must be your own leg) towards ze ball.

3) Hit your side of ze ball wiz ze foot, first making sure it is your own foot and it has a boot on it (if you use any uzzer part of your body it will not count).

4) Make sure ze ball goes between ze two upright posts and below ze top one, but NOT where ze goalie is standing (he is ze big fellow in ze different schirt von his team mates).

5) Und don't forget to follow srew. (No, I don't know what zis means eizer.)

6) If ze ball goes into ze net, you must jump about and shout.

7) If ze ball does NOT go into ze net, you must collapse onto ze ground and weep.

8) If you sink ze ball has gone into ze net, but ze referee does not agree wiz you, you must jump, shout, collapse and weep all at ze same time. If you are playing in South America, you will of course shoot ze referee.

Now we are going to get zis bloody right and turn ze boys into ze best schwingers in the world, ja? Und boys, do we need some good schwingers!

Und now, mit all ze stress of ze Euros, ze penalties and schwingers out of ze way, it's time for some *kalte bier* (ze German word for beer). But now zere is ein grosse dilemma... which beer to choose?

Should I be drinking ze beer zat is said to refresh ze parts uzzer biers cannot reach?

Or ze beer zay say is probably ze best in the world?

Or ze bier zat you never need to schkim?

Or ze one zat vurks vunders?

Or ze one where ze pint sinks it's a quart? (I blame ze decimalisation)

Or ze one where ze Australians wouldn't give a XXXX for anysing else?

Or ze one zat stays scharp to ze bottom of ze glass?

I am not zo sure. Zo for now, I vill stick
wiz my SCHMUSE–BEER, JA!

Oh Mein Gott – I zink I've had too many beers again. Zo, it's time to point Percy at ze porcelain, meine Schmuse-bears.

PS No peeking at my little pinkie (you naughty, naughty boys and girls)!

Zo after zese few biers I will need to get my curly bits done. (No sniggering at ze back you naughty, naughty people!) I am talking about meine BEARD. For zis I go to Billy, ze best barber I know. Billy ze Barber is in Museum Street, just around ze corner from ze London HQ of LFC in Bloomsbury.

Und now my Liverpool boys and girls and Schmuse-bears, now that I have had a few beers and all my bits done at Billy's I am ready to schtart ze kuchen, ja? Und guess what I'm gonna kuch…

Ze one and only SCOUSE!

Do you even know what ze word 'Scouser' really means? I will tell you, meine Schmuse-bears, because not a lot of people know zis!

Liverpool people are often called 'scousers' because zey eat scouse, a simple stew which you kuch wiz big chunks of meat, usually lamb or sometimes beef, wiz potatoes and onions and any leftovers you have to hand, such as your old football boots. Ze old Liverpool sailors used to eat it when zey arrived home from a long voyage when zey had had nussing to eat for months except ship's biscuits and rats.

Cheeky Jurgen's secret recipe for Scouse is in the videos below.

SCHHHHHHH.....

Now zat ze scouse is kuching in ze oven, Cheeky Jurgen has some other big secrets to reveal... turn ze pages to find out what zey are.

Cheeky Jurgen is a trained top horticulturalist and he certainly knows his turnips from his swedes, meine Schmuse-bears! (Unlike Jonathan Swain from Good Morning Britain, who doesn't know his Cheeky Jurgens from his Jurgen Klopps).

Cheeky Jurgen can teach you many things about how to grow the ingredients you will need for his scouse recipe.

Und just between me und you, meine schmuse-bears, Cheeky Jurgen's German is nicht zo gut...
On a visit to Germany many, many years ago, driving down ze autobahn from Belgium I saw a road sign: 'Ausfahrt'. Und zen 20k down the road ze same sign appeared and then 100k again ze same sign – 'Ausfahrt'. Oh mein Gott, I thought to myself, Ausfahrt must be a bloody big city, and I have never even heard of it!

At ziss stage, I realised also zat I had eggs-it on my face...

And now we are in ze first period of extra time...

(Ze publishers of ziss book insisted we had at least 100 pages... zay are such hard taskmasters. But I bet zey you are regretting it now, Toni, ja? I bet you zink zis book seems like it is going on forever!

So...
from..
now...
on...

We have to string ze words out a little, ja?

Now to Cheeky Jurgen's biggest secret. Zis will be a second page where Cheeky Jurgen has a serious point to make.

Wait for it…......

My name is not Cheeky Jurgen at all!

I bet that has surprised you, ja? I bet you are *erstaunt!* (That's 'astounded' in German.) My real name is Ray Cornwell. I was born and raised in New Cross, South East London, that's *Neue Kreuz, Sud Est…* oh forget it.). My local team is Millwall (the Lions). But enough of zis pretend German for now.

I, Ray, would like to share with you an inspiring and somewhat prophetic story. Some years ago, there was a game which I was lucky enough to be at where Millwall were playing Leicester City and Millwall won 1-0. I remember the singing directed at the Leicester City supporters: some Millwall fans were chanting 'You dirty northern b******s' and as a man of some education, I thought, geographically they are actually from the bloody Midlands, you crazy, wonderful Millwall supporters! (I love them dearly – even though they get a bad press. Perhaps it's because they get a bad press).

A big lesson I learnt from this is that it doesn't matter who you support;

If you follow your dreams and instincts, both in football and in life, you can achieve almost anything.

Only a few short years later, Leicester City were Champions of the Premier bloody League. So with regard to the six clubs who were trying to make a Super League, I think this is a good lesson to learn: that all the clubs in the various leagues deserve the chance and the possibility to progress and reach the very, very top.

(A really big thanks to Mr Klopp for being a true sportsman and spokesman for the fans and making it clear that he wasn't happy with this crazy proposal).

And now we go back to ze football for Cheeky's Jurgen's Observations and Predictions for the 2021/2022 *beste sechs*. No, that's not what you think it means – it means TOP SIX!

Sixth Place

TOTTENHAM HOTSPUR
The Lilywhites

It does not need to be said, with a nickname like this, they are not going to go very far. They need to dare some more, ja?

Fifth Place

CHELSEA
AKA The Pensioners

Ja, zay do play like a bunch of old men.
Even if zey are a RICH bunch of old men... living
off Russian money!

Fourth Place

MANCHESTER CITY
The Citizens

I think Man City are like Citizen Kane in the movie – a little dysfunctional, ja? All ze oil money in ze world can't buy class

Third Place

LEICESTER CITY
The Foxes

Ze lovely *silver* foxes. (I sink ze ladies and some gentlemen know what I mean). They have come zo far and have been such an inspiration for all the clubs below them (including my beloved Millwall). You are what the league is all about.

Second Place

MANCHESTER UNITED
The Red Devils

Our greatest ever rivalry. LFC and MUFC are
the two most successful clubs in English history.
MUFC: hated, adored, but never ignored.

TOP OF THE LEAGUE
And Premier League
Champions for the 20th Time:

LIVERPOOL
The Reds!

And I say this because I believe in it, I dream about it, but mainly because my bloody job depends on it. Please don't sack me yet, meine Schmusebears! (Jurgen's job and Cheeky's depend on this!)

ADDENDUM

Ziss is a very posh Latin word for time added on in extra time...

From Ray

(AKA Cheeky Jurgen)

I am actually mildly dyslexic. I know, I know, you would never guess that from this wonderful work of literature you have been reading!

If you have read this far, of course... if you have, thank you.

I was an underachiever at school and left at the age of sixteen. I started with very little, but I was lucky and through hard work, perseverance and dedication I was able to enjoy a little success.

But never in a million years did I envisage the crazy wild journey of the last year or so and the possibility of ever writing a book, but with the help of my friends and the initial inspiration of my adorable and unique granddaughter Annabella I did it.

'Pappi, Pappi, why are you always on TV?'

This book would not have been possible without…
THANKS AND CREDITS

1. My dear, darling, diva Annabella for giving me the original 'sliding doors' moment for Cheeky Jurgen.

2. The other diva in my life: Patsy Prince. (Hated, adored but never ignored). Friend, confidante and Cheeky's Manager.

3. Our fabulous illustrator Josh Knowles.

4. Geraldine Beskin of the Atlantis Bookshop, who accosted me in the street after seeing Cheeky Jurgen's antics with the suggestion of: "Why not write a book?"

5. Billy the barber in Bloomsbury who trims my bits and makes me look just like Jurgen.

6. That bloke in The Crown PH and Fangs FX for getting the teeth absolutely perfect.

7. Jonathan Swain at ITV for making an honest mistake which accidentally gave us more publicity than we could ever have dreamt of.

8. Tiff and The Hamster Hammond for being such good sports at the London Classic Car Show.

9. My Schumuse-Dog for falling for me in the street.

10. All the Liverpool boys and girls especially Neil and Craig at DTBTV for giving Patsy and I such a warm Scouse welcome on our visit to Liverpool and the confidence to take Cheeky Jurgen to the next level.

11. All the rest of my family and friends who have put up with my eccentric craziness for many, many years which has culminated in the one and only Cheeky Jurgen.

12. John Pearman and everyone involved with 'Red All Over The Land' for that first interview.

13. Russell Selwyn, my football loving and long-lunch adoring friend and accountant, who says (hopefully), that he has set up a 'scheme' that gives me the artistic licence to be quite cheeky and funny but without the worry of going to prison. (We will see).

And last but certainly not least the real man himself Mr Jurgen Klopp whom has probably had several raised eyebrows at some of my goings on and has always been such a sport.

PS: Enormous thanks to the gang at Mereo Books. Especially Antonia Tingle (Ms) – who never doubted us or ceases to surprise.

I hope you enjoyed this book and joining me on this crazy lovely journey. As a thank you I would like to offer you 25% off your bill at any of the Cheeky Chico's Mexican restaurants in London that I helped found several years ago. Please bring this book and show this page at any Cheeky Chico's and the staff will give you a Cheeky Stamp to validate it.
You never know, I might even be there to share a Cheeky moment with you.

Printed in Great Britain
by Amazon